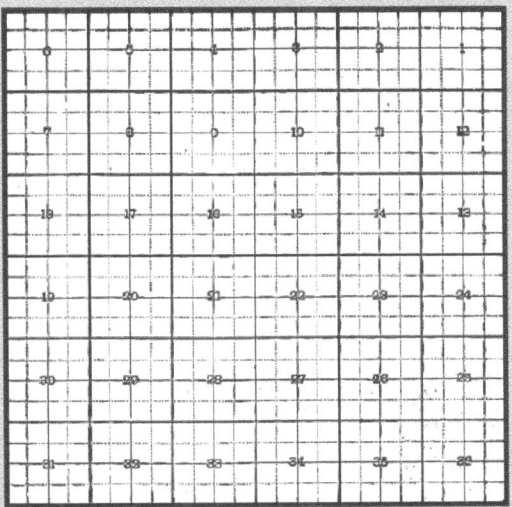

Above: Since 1785 Federal land surveyors used the township as the major subdivision of the public domain under the rectangular system of surveys. Townships are approximately 6 miles on each side and contain 36 sections of 640 acres apiece, numbered in the sequence above. Sections are further subdivided into half, quarter, and lesser sections, called aliquot parts. A township is identified by its relation to a base line and principal meridian, e.g., township 7 south, range 26 west, Sixth Principal Meridian (6th PM).

Front cover: "A 'close-up' of a homesteader's house of the better type, showing one of the 'sure crops.'" Record Group 49, Records of the Bureau of Land Management, General Land Office, Field Service Division, Santa Fe, New Mexico.

Back cover: The engraving that appeared on patent documents for land entries under the Homestead Act of 1862.

Research in the Land Entry Files
of the General Land Office

RECORD GROUP 49

COMPILED BY KENNETH HAWKINS

REFERENCE INFORMATION PAPER 114

National Archives and Records Administration, Washington, DC

Revised 2009

The National Archives and Records Administration (NARA) is the official repository for records of the U.S. General Land Office, a predecessor of the Bureau of Land Management, that document the transfer of public lands from the United States to private ownership.[1] The case files generated by over 10 million such individual land transactions, known as land entries, and the tract books and various name indexes used to access them are located in the National Archives Building, Washington, DC.

NARA has custody of the land entry case files for the 30 Federal public land states. There are case files for all states in the United States **except** the original 13 states, Vermont, Kentucky, Tennessee, Maine, West Virginia, Texas, and Hawaii. These states were never part of the original public domain.[2]

INFORMATION FOUND IN LAND ENTRY CASE FILES

These files can contain a wealth of genealogical and legal information. Depending upon the type and time period of land entry, the case file may yield only a few facts already known to the researcher, or it may present new insights about ancestors, family history, title, and land use issues. Case files for land entries made before the 1840s may contain only schematic information such as the name of the entryman; the land's location, acreage, and price; and the date and place of the land entry. Or they may, in cases of military bounty land warrants and private land claims, establish a record of U.S. military service or reveal that the claimant settled a location before it was annexed by the United States. Case files for land entries made after about 1840 under the Cash Act (1820), Preemption acts (1830s–1840s), Donation Act (1850), Homestead Act (1862), Mineral acts (1860s–1870s), Timber Culture Act (1873), Desert Land Act (1877), and several military bounty land warrant acts (1840s–1850s) generally include more information. The records can attest to the entryman's age, place of birth, citizenship, military service, literacy, and economic status, among other vital

---

[1] **Please note:** Federal land records document only the **FIRST** transfer of title to land from the United States to another party. Records of later transfers may be found in county or state records. Contact the appropriate county recorder of deeds, state archives, or historical society.

[2] Some of the original colonies and eastern states also sold land and awarded military bounty land warrants on their own. Researchers interested in such records should contact the appropriate state archives or historical society.

information, and sometimes include similar information about family members. They also provide evidence of first title and occasionally of land use, rights-of-ways, survey lines, crops and improvements, archeological imprints, and conflicting claims.

Such information is not guaranteed to be in every land entry case file. Over 40 separate legislative acts were used by Americans to make a land entry on the public lands, and each act required different information from the entryman. Thus the documentation available in the land entry case file depends largely upon the legal requirements of the act under which the land entry was made. Used imaginatively, however, even the smallest case files can establish locations of land ownership or settlement and dates essential to exploit other resources at NARA, such as census, court, and military service and pension records.

This publication is intended to provide an overview of the land entry files held at the National Archives Building and an introduction to research in them. It cannot begin to detail the many additional records of the General Land Office (GLO) that relate to land entries and land use available to researchers at the National Archives Building and NARA's regional records services facilities. For more detailed information on land records, please see Robert Kvasnicka's *The Trans-Mississippi West, 1804–1912, Part IV, Section 3, Records of the General Land Office* (Washington, DC: National Archives Trust Fund, to be published in 2007).

ARRANGEMENT AND ACCESS[3]

Land entry case files comprise the paperwork accumulated by a local U.S. land office in administering a land entry application. Once the legal requirements governing a land entry were met, whether by a cash payment, surrender of a bounty land warrant, or proof of residency and improvements, officials at the local land office forwarded the case file to the headquarters of the GLO in Washington, DC, along with a final certificate that declared it eligible for a patent. There the case file was examined, and if found valid, a patent or deed of title for the land was sent back to the local land office for delivery to the entryman. The GLO also recorded each land entry in tract books

---

[3] Researchers may wish to consult the tabular searchpaths printed at the end of this pamphlet.

arranged by state and legal description of the land in terms of numbered section, township, and range. The case files were retained and kept in separate filing systems for military bounty land warrants, pre-1908 general land entry files, and post-1908 general land entry files.

The United States issued bounty land warrants to attract enlistments during the Revolutionary War, the War of 1812, and the Mexican War and to reward service in these conflicts and in a variety of Indian wars, Indian removal, and other military actions during the 1850s. The GLO filed most of the military bounty land warrant case files by the year of the congressional act that authorized them, the number of acres granted, and the warrant number. These three elements of information are required to identify and retrieve these files. Name indices and other means to access these files are discussed below in the section on military bounty land warrants.

Before July 1908, the GLO kept the case files for all general land entries according to state, land office, type of entry (such as credit, cash, homestead, timber, and mineral), and final certificate number (sometimes called the file or document number). Large portions of the pre-July 1908 land entry case files are not indexed by name. Selected name indices and other methods to obtain the information required to identify and retrieve the case files are discussed below.

After July 1908, the GLO filed all general land entries regardless of state or type in one large series by serial patent number. Name indices that provide the patent number of all post-July 1908 land entries are available in the National Archives Building through the mid 1950s when NARA holdings taper off. For serial land patents after the mid 1950s, it may be necessary to contact the relevant contemporary Bureau of Land Management (BLM) district office for the state in question.

A name index to the pre-July 1908 general land entry case files, maintained on file cards, is available for **Alabama, Alaska, Arizona, Florida, Louisiana, Nevada,** and **Utah**. Called the "Seven States Index,"[4] it shows the entryman's name, state in which the land was located, land office where the entry was made, type of entry, and final certificate or file number. It thus supplies all four of the information elements needed to have a land entry case file retrieved or "pulled" for examination. It also shows the legal

---

[4] Seven States Index, RG 49, Master Location Register number (MLR #) UD168.

description of the land in terms of numbered section, township, and range. The Seven States Index includes both successful land entries that received patents and unsuccessful land entries, also called canceled or relinquished land entries, which did not receive patents. NARA has case files for both patented and unpatented land entries before 1908.

The four information elements noted above are also required to retrieve pre-July 1908 general land entry files for the remaining 23 public land states. Some researchers may already have possession of this information because they have a copy of the U.S. patent issued for the land. Those who do not have this information must obtain it from the General Land Office tract books or other sources. The present location of these tract books depends on whether the GLO's successor agency, the Bureau of Land Management, categorized the public land states as "eastern" or "western":

Eastern	*Western*
Alabama	Alaska
Arkansas	Arizona
Florida	California
Illinois	Colorado
Indiana	Idaho
Iowa	Kansas
Louisiana	Montana
Michigan	Nebraska
Minnesota	Nevada
Mississippi	New Mexico
Missouri	North Dakota
Ohio	Oklahoma
Wisconsin	Oregon
	South Dakota
	Utah
	Washington
	Wyoming

GLO tract books for the 17 western public land states listed above are held at the National Archives Building in Washington, DC. A map index to each state's tract books allows researchers to identify the tract book number that covers the area in which they are interested. Some GLO tract books are held by NARA's regional records services facilities and occasionally by other repositories in western public land states. See "Using the Tract Books" below.

The Eastern State Office of the Bureau of Land Management (BLM-ESO), 7450 Boston Boulevard, Springfield, VA 22153, has retained custody of the GLO tract books for the 13 eastern public land states. The BLM-ESO also has a computerized index of patented land entries for all public land states post-1820, excluding land patents prior to 1908 located in Montana, Nebraska, and Oklahoma. This index is on the BLM web site at *www.glo-records.blm.gov*. Complete entries from this index give the information needed to locate given case files at NARA. Land offices and types of land entries are given for some states in the system as code numbers, and the final certificate number is designated the "document number."

Since GLOARS covers only patented entries, it does not serve as an index to pre-1820 entries (with some sporadic exceptions regarding land warrants) and the many thousands of canceled or relinquished land case files generated in the course of the Federal public land business. Such case files often have as much information useful to the researcher as those of patented entries. To obtain file information on cancelled entries in the eastern states, researchers much consult the headquarters tract books of the GLO tract books in the custody of the Bureau of Land Management's Eastern States Office. Tract books used by branch offices of the GLO may be held by state repositories in public land states, but these are not as authoritative as the central office tract books held respectively by the BLM and NARA.

USING THE TRACT BOOKS AT THE NATIONAL ARCHIVES BUILDING

These large bound volumes document all general and bounty land warrant land entries before and after 1908 and provide the information elements needed to identify and retrieve land entry case files for examination. The information recorded includes the type of land entry; its legal description in terms of numbered section, township, and range; its acreage and price; the name of the entryman; date of application and/or patenting; and the final certificate, serial patent, or warrant number. The tract books also contain additional information affecting all land entries in a given area, such as the local land office handling entries, rights of way, forest reserves,

Indian reservations, and state lands.

The tract books are arranged by numbered section, township, and range in what is termed a "legal description" of the land. In order to use the tract books effectively, the researcher must know the legal description of the land parcel in which they are interested. Civil divisions such as counties and named townships were not used by the GLO and therefore are of limited use to the researcher using its records. Legal description of land can usually be obtained from the county recorder of deeds and is shown also on some commercial atlases. For more information on the legal description of land, see "A Note on Cadastral Surveys" below.

To identify the number of the tract book covering any given piece of land in a western public land state, the researcher should consult the tract book index map for that state.[5] Each map shows the principal meridian and base line governing land surveys in the state, as well as the numbered townships and ranges that appear as a grid covering the entire state. The researcher will locate the appropriate numbered township and range for their area and find that it is included with a group of others in a block designated by a tract book volume number. The researcher should request that tract book by state and volume number.

Once the tract book is in hand, the researcher can locate the record of the land entry under the appropriate numbered section, township, and range listed on the left side of each page in the volume. Each land entry was recorded in the tract book across two pages. Once the record of the land entry is located, the researcher must extract the information needed to retrieve and examine the land entry case file.

REQUESTING THE LAND ENTRY CASE FILE

Each request for a land entry case file must include the following information elements: **Pre-July 1908** general land entries require the *state, land office, type of land entry,* and *final certificate number.* **Post-July 1908** general land entries require *name of entryman* and *serial patent number.* **Bounty land warrants** require the *year of the congressional act authorizing the war-*

---

[5] Index to Tract Books, RG 49, MLR# UD2321, maps arranged by state. Copies of these maps are available for consultation in room G-28 of the National Archives Building, Washington, DC.

Tract book illustration 1

Tract book illustration 2

rant, acreage, and *warrant number.* The location of each of these within the tract book entry is illustrated on page 7.[6]

1. The **type of land entry** was usually abbreviated in the far left column: Homestead entries were abbreviated as "Hd," "H.E.," or "Home." Cash entries were "P.a." or "Pre. 41," for the preemption act of 1841, or "cash." Timber Culture entries were "T.C." Desert entries were "D.E." Military bounty land warrant entries were routinely cited on either the left or right tract book page and varied in format but always included the year of the act authorizing the warrant, the acreage, and the warrant number. (Also shown: the legal description of the land entries, the acreage, price or fees paid, and the name of the entryman.) **Enter the type of entry on your request form.**

2. The **final certificate** or **patent number** is located in different parts of the right tract book page, depending on the type of land entry and its disposition. If it was a cash or preemption entry, the file number was usually recorded under the column headed "Number of receipt and certificate of purchase." If it was a Homestead Act, Timber Culture Act, or Desert Land Act entry, this column was used for the application number.[7] The file number for these types of entries was usually entered under the "By Whom Patented" or "Date of Patent" columns as the final certificate, "F.C.," or patent, "Pat.," number. **Enter the appropriate number on your request form.**

3. Because the pre-July 1908 general land entry case files are arranged by type and number under the name of the land office, it is essential that the correct land office be cited in any request for these files. Each state had up to a dozen different land offices for various areas and time periods. The land office that administered the land entry was sometimes listed on the right tract book page, near the final certificate or patent number. In cases where the land office was not cited in the tract book, researchers can consult an index prepared by the GLO that is arranged by state, meridian, township, and range and chronicles the time periods during which various land offices administered the public lands in any given area.[8] **Enter the appropriate land office on your request form.**

---

[6] Kansas, tract book vol. 75, p. 35, for sections 31 and 32, township 7 south, range 26 west.
[7] For Homestead Act, Timber Culture, and Desert Land land entries, the application number became the final filing number only if the land entry was canceled, relinquished, or commuted to a cash entry by purchase. Such dispositions were recorded on the right-hand page of the tract book. Land entry case files so noted should be requested as such.
[8] Index to Land Offices, 4 vols., MLR# UD2320.

When these information elements are obtained, correct requests for pre-1908 land entry case files from the Oberlin, Kansas, land office would read like this:

Kansas, Oberlin land office, Homestead final certificate #4758
   [Gottlieb Sandmeier]

Kansas, Oberlin land office, cash entry #4111 [Charles W. Little]

Kansas, Oberlin land office, canceled Homestead #17115 [John W.
   Gordon]

Kansas, Oberlin land office, Timber Culture final certificate #1274
   [William Flesher]

Land entries patented after 1908 do not require citation of the land office to retrieve the case file; they require only the patent number. A post-1908 serial land patent entry from the same land office might read:

Serial Land Patent No. 64998 [Henry A. Russell]

Learning what information elements are required to retrieve a land entry case file and entering them correctly on the request form, without extraneous or incomplete information, will enhance the accuracy and efficiency of the retrieval and research process.

A NOTE ON CADASTRAL SURVEYS

The cadastral elements of principal meridian, numbered section, township, and range governed the survey and disposition of the public lands in the United States. As each territory or state came within the public domain, the GLO established a base line running east and west and a principal meridian north and south to guide land surveys. Numbered townships were laid out in tiers north and south of the base line while numbered ranges were laid out east and west of the meridians. The intersecting lines of townships and ranges formed a checkerboard or grid of townships, each containing 36 sections. Each section of a township contains 640 acres and is 1 square mile in area. Typical land entries consisted of parcels between 40 acres and 320 or more acres, usually in increments of 20 acres. NARA has original GLO survey notes for Illinois, Indiana, Iowa, Kansas, Missouri, and Ohio and original GLO township plats for Alabama, Illinois, Indiana, Iowa, Kansas, Mississippi, Missouri, Oklahoma, Wisconsin, and

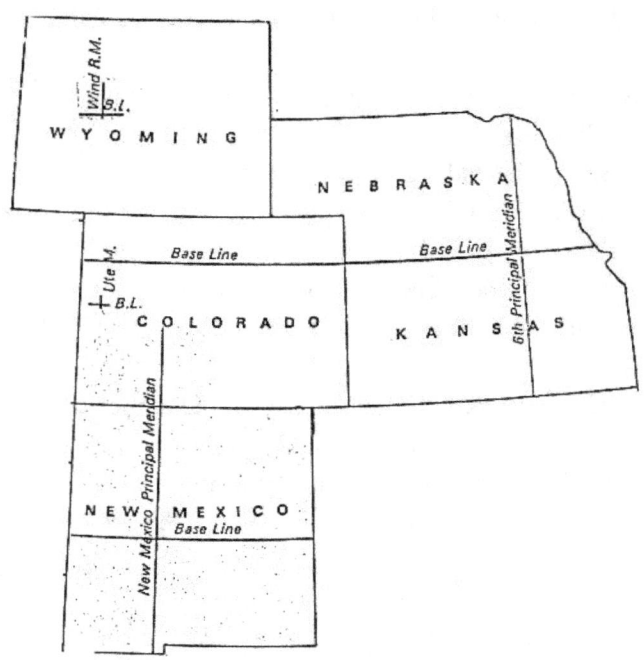

parts of Ohio. They are reproduced in NARA microfilm publications **T1240** and **T1234**, described in the microfilm section. Survey notes and plats for other public land states generally are held by the Bureau of Land Management, (BLM) Eastern States Office, and various BLM state offices.

Often the public lands of one or more states are governed by a single principal meridian. For example, all of Kansas and Nebraska and most of Wyoming and Colorado base their land surveys on the Sixth Principal Meridian (6th PM).

The base line of the 6th PM forms the state boundary between Kansas and Nebraska so townships north of the baseline are in Nebraska, and those south of it are in Kansas. The 6th PM divides Kansas and Nebraska into eastern and western segments. Thus one location in northeast Nebraska is described as township 27 north, range 5 east, 6th PM. One in east Kansas is township 27 south, range 5 east, 6th PM. Similarly, two locations in the western parts of each state are, respectively, township 27 north, range 5 west (Nebraska), and township 27 south, range 5 west (Kansas). Except for parts of Wyoming controlled by the Wind River Meridian and parts of Colorado governed by the New Mexico Meridian, all townships in Wyoming are also north of the baseline of the 6th PM; most townships in Colorado are south of its baseline; and all ranges in both Wyoming and Colorado are west of the 6th PM. Most good commercial atlases show meridians, baselines, townships, and ranges.

MILITARY BOUNTY LAND WARRANTS

From 1788 to 1855 the United States granted military bounty land warrants for military service. At the time of the Revolutionary War, the United States and several of the original states used land bounties to attract enlistments; the United States used the same incentive during the War of 1812. Most of these early U.S. warrants could only be used in military districts, for lands now principally in Ohio and several other eastern and central public land states. Most of the Revolutionary War bounty land warrants were sold or assigned by the soldiers or warrantees to others. Between 1847 and 1855 the Government granted a series of increasingly generous land bounties, first to attract enlistments in the Mexican War, then to reward surviving veterans of all wars since 1790 (including Indian wars), and finally to include those who served in the Revolutionary War. Under the acts of the 1850s, eligibility was gradually extended to include the regular army, navy, militia, and Indians mustered into the service of the United States. The majority of those who received warrants under the acts of 1847–55, did not use them to make land entries themselves but sold them to others who did. These warrants could be used to obtain land anywhere in the public domain. Most bounty land warrant acts allowed, in the event of the death of those eligible, for the warrants to be issued to their immediate heirs. No land bounties were offered to Civil War veterans, but Union soldiers could deduct the time they served from the residency requirements of the Homestead Act of 1862.

At the National Archives Building, NARA has custody of those military bounty land warrants that were used or surrendered to the Federal Government in exchange for land. They are arranged by the year of the act of Congress that authorized them, the certificate or warrant number, and, for warrants under the acts of 1847–55, by the number of acres granted. There are name indexes for the Revolutionary War, most of the War of 1812 warrants, and some of the warrants under the acts of 1847–55.

Although many of the earliest warrants were lost in fires at the War Department, surviving warrants issued for service in the Revolutionary War are reproduced and indexed in NARA microfilm publications **M829** and **M804**, described below in the microfilm section. There is also a card index to them in the National Archives Building,[9] and they are indexed in the following publications, which are available at most large public, university or genealogical libraries:

Clifford Neal Smith, *Federal Bounty-Land Warrants of the American Revolution, 1799–1835* (Chicago: American Library Association, 1973).

National Genealogical Society, *Index of Revolutionary War Pension [and Bounty-Land Warrant] Applications in the National Archives* (Washington, DC: National Genealogical Society, 1976).

Surviving veterans of the Revolutionary War also qualified for bounty land warrants under the act of 1855. These are partially indexed in NARA microfilm publication **M804**, described below in the microfilm section, and the second publication cited above.

WAR OF 1812 BOUNTY LAND WARRANTS

The earliest bounty land warrants for service in the War of 1812, issued at the time of the war, are partially reproduced and indexed in NARA microfilm publications **M848** and **M313**, described below in the microfilm section.

Surviving veterans of the War of 1812 also qualified for bounty land warrants under the acts of 1842, 1850, 1852, and 1855. These warrants are indexed in NARA microfilm publications **M848** and **M313**, described below in the microfilm section. They are also partially indexed in the following publication:

Virgil D. White, *Index to War of 1812 Pension [and Bounty-Land Warrant] Files,* 3 vols. (Waynesboro, TN: National Historical Publishing Company, 1989).

---

[9] Alphabetical Index to U.S. Revolutionary War Bounty Land Warrants, Act of July 9, 1788, MLR# UD2139.

Surviving veterans of the various Indian wars since 1790 qualified for bounty land warrants under the acts of 1850–55. These are partially indexed (for military actions against Indians during the War of 1812 only) in NARA microfilm publication **M313**, described in the microfilm section. Warrants issued for other military actions against Indians are indexed by the warrant applications under these acts, discussed below.

MEXICAN WAR BOUNTY LAND WARRANTS

The United States under an act of 1847 issued bounty land warrants to encourage enlistments in the Mexican War. Warrants under this act were the first that could be used to enter land anywhere in the public domain (rather than limiting entry to military districts) and were assignable. They are indexed in the NARA microfilm publication **T317**, described below in the microfilm section.

BOUNTY LAND WARRANTS UNDER THE ACTS OF 1850, 1852, AND 1855

Under the acts of 1850, 1852, and 1855, Congress gradually extended the eligibility for bounty land warrants to retroactively compensate surviving veterans or the immediate heirs of all who had served since the Revolutionary War, as noted above. Those who obtained warrants under an earlier act usually were eligible under later acts as well, provided the total acreage they obtained did not exceed 160 acres. The card, microfilm, and published indexes cited above, while valuable, do not include references to each of the hundreds of thousands of veterans, widows, and survivors who obtained bounty land warrants under the acts of 1850–55. The most comprehensive "index" to determine information about the filing of these warrants is the bounty land warrant application files among the military pension records held by NARA, most of which have not been microfilmed.[10] Researchers who are unable to locate bounty land warrant filing information using the indexes noted above

---

[10] Note: bounty land warrant application files usually contain more information useful to the researcher than do the surrendered warrants.

should use NATF Form 85, Order for Copies of Federal Pension or Bounty Land Warrant Applications, to request a copy of the land warrant *application.* Each approved application will note the filing information of the surrendered warrant, given as a three-part number containing the warrant number, the acreage granted, and the year of the act granting the warrant. For example, warrant number 12345 for 160 acres, granted under the act of 1855, would read: "12345-160-1855," "12345-160-'55," or some variation thereof. This filing information should then be cited when requesting the surrendered bounty land warrant file. Since there are thousands of surrendered warrants under each acreage group of these acts, it is important to include all three parts of the filing information in a request.

MILITARY BOUNTY LAND WARRANTS, LAND ENTRY CASE FILES, AND GENERAL LAND OFFICE ADMINISTRATIVE RECORDS AVAILABLE ON MICROFILM

Because NARA holds approximately 10 million pre-July 1908 case files for land entries and military bounty land warrants, it is not feasible to microfilm or scan them all. Limited series of these files have been microfilmed and are available across the country at the regional facilities of NARA and other repositories. Several of these microfilm publications have useful and informative guides that describe the records and how to access them. Several also contain the filing information needed to request copies of the surrendered bounty land warrant and pre-July 1908 general land entry case files. Inquiries about these and other land-related microfilm publications may be directed to the Old Military and Civil Records (NWCTB), National Archives and Records Administration, Washington, DC 20408. *Please note that the paper originals of microfilmed records are no longer available for copying; reproductions are made from the microfilm.*

1. *U.S. Revolutionary War Bounty Land Warrants Used in the U.S. Military District of Ohio and Related Papers (Acts of 1788, 1803, and 1806).* **M829**. 16 rolls. This publication indexes and reproduces all the warrants under these acts that survived fires in the War Department buildings in 1800 and 1814.

2. *Revolutionary War Pension and Bounty-Land Warrant Application Files.* **M804**. 2,670 rolls. This publication indexes bounty land warrants

for Revolutionary War service under the early acts noted above and under the act of 1855. It reproduces the complete applications for approved bounty land warrants under the act of 1855 only.

3. *War of 1812 Military Bounty Land Warrants, 1815–1858.* **M848.** 14 rolls. This publication partially indexes bounty land warrants under the acts of 1812, 1814, and 1842 only, not later acts. It reproduces the stubs retained by the Federal Government for issued warrants; the warrants that were used, or surrendered, have not been filmed. They are filed by the warrant number given in this microfilm publication and are described under entries 13 and 14 in National Archives Preliminary Inventory 22, *Land-Entry Papers of the General Land Office.*

4. *Index to War of 1812 Pension Application Files.* **M313.** 102 rolls. This gives, in the upper right-hand corner of each entry, the filing information for bounty land warrants granted under the acts of 1812, 1850, and 1855. Warrants under the act of 1850 include those for service in various Indian wars since 1790.

5. *Index to Mexican War Pension Files, 1887–1926.* **T317.** 14 rolls. This index gives filing information for bounty land warrants granted under the act of 1847.

6. *List of North Carolina Land Grants in Tennessee, 1778–1791.* **M68.** 1 roll. The volume reproduced on the single roll of this microfilm publication was prepared in the Office of the Secretary of State of North Carolina in 1791 and submitted the same year to Thomas Jefferson, Secretary of State of the United States. It is not indexed. Lands in North Carolina and Tennessee were never part of the Federal public domain; therefore, the General Land Office had no jurisdiction over land transactions in those states. Inquiries should be addressed to the respective state archives.

7. *Oregon and Washington Donation Land Files, 1851–1903.* **M815.** 108 rolls. These land claims, like most general land entries before 1908, are arranged by state, land office, and final certificate number. This microfilm publication reproduces the case files for each approved claim under the Donation Land Act of 1850. Name indexes are available in the NARA microfilm publications, *Abstracts of Oregon Donation Land Claims, 1852–1903,* **M145,** 6 rolls, and *Abstracts of*

Washington Donation Land Claims, 1855–1902, **M203,** 1 roll. A published name index and abstract is available.

8. *Bound Records of the General Land Office Relating to Private Land Claims in Louisiana, 1767–1892.* **M1382.** 8 rolls. Roll 2 includes "Old Index of Private Land Claims in Louisiana, 1800–1880." Individual case files of these claims are not included in this microfilm publication.

9. *Unbound Records of the General Land Office Relating to Private Land Claims in Louisiana, 1805–1896.* **M1385.** 2 rolls.

10. *Land Claims Case Files of the U.S. District Court for the Eastern District of Louisiana, 1844–1880.* **M1115.** 16 rolls.

11. *Records Relating to California Private Land Claims Dockets.* **T910.** 118 rolls. An alphabetical index by grant title is found on roll 118. Lists by name of grantee are found at the start of each roll. Indexes by both grant name and grantee name are available.

12. *Index to Private Land Grant Cases, U.S. District Court, Northern District of California, 1853–1903.* **T1214.** 1 roll. The records in this and the following three microfilm publications document court cases relating to private land claims in California. They may include information from General Land Office docketed case files as well as records relating to the proceedings of cases in the U.S. district courts.

13. *Index to Private Land Grant Cases, U.S. District Court, Southern District of California.* **T1215.** 1 roll.

14. *Index by County to Private Land Grant Cases, U.S. District Court, Northern and Southern Districts of California.* **T1216.** 1 roll.

15. *Private Land Grant Case Files in the Circuit Court of the Northern District of California, 1852–1910.* **T1207.** 28 rolls.

16. *Federal Land Records for Idaho, 1860–1934.* **M1620.** 23 rolls. Includes registers of land entries kept by local land offices; original tract books.

17. *Federal Land Records for Oregon, 1854–1908.* **M1621.** 92 rolls. Includes registers, abstracts of land entries kept by local land offices and tract books.

18. *Federal Land Records for Washington, 1860–1910.* **M1622.** 72 rolls. Includes registers, abstracts of land entries kept by local land offices and tract books.

19. *Records of the Bureau of Land Management, Surveyor General of*

Arizona, 1891–1950. **M1627**. 2 rolls. Includes records relating to survey requests and surveyor personnel records.

20. *Records of the Bureau of Land Management, Phoenix General Land Office, 1873–1942.* **M1628**. 15 rolls. Selected registers of land entries kept by local land offices.

21. *Records of the Bureau of Land Management, Prescott General Land Office, 1871–1908.* **M1629**. 16 rolls. Selected registers of land entries kept by local land offices and land entry decisions.

22. *Records of the Bureau of Land Management, Los Angeles District Land Office, 1859–1936.* **M1630**. 60 rolls. Selected registers of land entries; declarations of intention to make land entries kept by local land offices and selected land entry case files arranged alphabetically.

23. *Miscellaneous Letters Sent by the General Land Office, 1796–1889.* **M25**. 228 rolls.

24. *Letters Sent by the General Land Office to the Surveyor General, 1796–1901.* **M27**. 31 rolls.

25. *Letters Sent by the Surveyor General of the Territory Northwest of the Ohio River, 1797–1854.* **M477**. 10 rolls.

26. *Letters Received by the Secretary of the Treasury and the Commissioner of the General Land Office From the Surveyor General of the Territory Northwest of the River Ohio, 1797–1849.* **M478**. 10 rolls.

27. *Letters Received by the Surveyor General of the Territory Northwest of the River Ohio, 1797–1856.* **M479**. 43 rolls.

28. *Township Plats of Selected States.* **T1234**. 62 rolls. Original GLO manuscript plats of townships in Alabama, Illinois, Indiana, Iowa, Kansas, Mississippi, Missouri, Oklahoma, Wisconsin, and parts of Ohio. Arranged by state and thereunder by principal meridian and numbered township and range. A roll list is available.

29. *Field Notes From Selected General Land Office Township Surveys.* **T1240**. 280 rolls. Survey field notes from the original GLO surveys of Illinois, Indiana, Iowa, Kansas, Missouri, and Ohio. Arranged by state and thereunder by volume number. Index maps for each state are reproduced at the front of each reel and provide the volume number in which survey notes for any given township and range are reproduced. The notes within each volume are arranged by numbered township and range. A roll list is available.

30. *Correspondence of the Surveyors General of Utah, 1874–1916.* **M1110.** 86 rolls.

31. *Correspondence Received by the Surveyors General of New Mexico, 1854–1907.* **M1288.** 11 rolls.

32. *Letters and Surveying Contracts Received by the General Land Office from the Surveyor General for Illinois, Missouri, and Arkansas, 1813–1832.* **M1323.** 2 rolls.

33. *Letters and Surveying Contracts Received by the General Land Office from the Surveyor General for Alabama, 1817–1832.* **M1325.** 1 roll.

34. *Letters Received by the Secretary of the Treasury and the General Land Office from the Surveyor General of Mississippi, 1803–1831.* **M1329.** 4 rolls.

35. *Letters Received by the Secretary of the Treasury Relating to Public Lands ("N" Series) 1831–1849.* **M726.** 23 rolls

36. *Letters Sent by the Secretary of the Treasury Relating to Public Lands ("N" Series), 1801–1878.* **M733.** 4 rolls.

ADDITIONAL READING

Thomas Donaldson, *The Public Domain. Its history, with statistics . . .* (Washington, DC: 1881, reprinted 1971).

Paul W. Gates, *History of Public Land Law Development* (Washington, DC: Government Printing Office, 1968).

W. Wade Hone, *Land and Property Research in the United States* (Salt Lake City: Ancestry, Inc., 1997).

Roy M. Robbins, *Our Landed Heritage: The Public Domain, 1776–1936* (Lincoln: University of Nebraska Press, 1962).

Malcom J. Rohrbough, *The Land Office Business; the Settlement and Administration of American Public Lands, 1789–1837* (New York: Oxford University Press, 1968).

Searchpaths for Requests by Mail

To obtain copies of case file of a:	Use one NATF Form 84 per file	Where to send completed forms
Land entry after July 1908	Use NATF Form 84, fill in state and name of entryman	Send to Textual Reference (NWCT1R), National Archives, 700 Pennsylvania Ave NW, Washington, DC 20408-0001
Land entry before July 1908 and in western[1] state	Use NATF Form 84, fill in state, name of entryman, and legal description of land	Send to Textual Reference (NWCT1R), National Archives, 700 Pennsylvania Ave NW, Washington, DC 20408-0001
Land entry before July 1908 and in eastern[2] state	Write to BLM-ESO[3] and get a copy of patent or record that shows state, land office, type of entry, and file number. Or consult BLM-ESO web site at *www.glorecords.blm.gov*	Use NATF Form 84, fill in state, land office, type of entry, and file number. Send to address given above
Land entry before July 1908, and you have patent from BLM-ESO, or you know state, land office, type of entry, and file number	Use NATF Form 84, fill in state, land office, type of land entry, and file number. Complete rest of form as needed	Send to Textual Reference (NWCT1R), National Archives, 700 Pennsylvania Ave NW, Washington, DC 20408-0001

---

[1] Alaska, Arizona, California, Colorado, Idaho, Kansas, Montana, Nebraska, Nevada, New Mexico, North Dakota, Oklahoma, Oregon, South Dakota, Utah, Washington, and Wyoming.
[2] Alabama, Arkansas, Florida, Illinois, Indiana, Iowa, Louisiana, Michigan, Minnesota, Mississippi, Missouri, Ohio, and Wisconsin.
[3] Bureau of Land Management, Eastern States Office, 7450 Boston Boulevard, Springfield, VA 22153.

Searchpaths for Requests by Mail

To obtain copies of warrant under Act of	Sources below index case files	Use one NATF Form 84 per file	Where to send completed forms
July 9, 1788 March 3, 1803 & April 15, 1806 **Revolutionary War service**	Entire series on NARA microfilm M829, arranged alphabetically. See also published indices[1]	Use NATF Form 84, fill in name of warrantee, year of warrant act, acreage, warrant number	Send to Textual Reference (NWCT1R), National Archives, 700 Pennsylvania Ave NW, Washington, DC 20408-0001
Dec. 24, 1811 Jan. 11, 1812 May 6, 1812 & July 27, 1842 **War of 1812 service**	Indexed and partially reproduced on NARA microfilm M848. See also published indices[2]	Use NATF Form 84, fill in name of warrantee, year of warrant act, acreage, warrant number	Send to Textual Reference (NWCT1R), National Archives, 700 Pennsylvania Ave NW, Washington, DC 20408-0001
February 11, 1847 **Mexican War service**	Indexed by NARA microfilm T317 and by warrant applications ordered with NATF Form 85	Use NATF Form 84, fill in name of warrantee, year of warrant act, acreage, warrant number.	Send to Textual Reference (NWCT1R), National Archives, 700 Pennsylvania Ave NW, Washington, DC 20408-0001
Sept. 28, 1850 March 22, 1852 **Service in all wars since 1790, including Indian Wars**	Warrants for 1812 service indexed by NARA microfilm M313. Others by warrant applications ordered with NATF Form 85. Published indices may be available	Use NATF Form 84, fill in name of warrantee, year of warrant act, acreage, warrant number.	Send to Textual Reference (NWCT1R), National Archives, 700 Pennsylvania Ave NW, Washington, DC 20408-0001
March 3, 1855 **Service in all wars including Revolutionary War**	Warrants for Rev. War service indexed by NARA microfilm M804. Others same as previous category	Use NATF Form 84, fill in name of warrantee, year of warrant act, acreage, warrant number	Send to Textual Reference (NWCT1R), National Archives, 700 Pennsylvania Ave NW, Washington, DC 20408-0001

Note: You can request a copy of a military bounty land *application* file by using the Form NATF 85, Order for Copies of Federal Pension or Bounty Land Warrant Applications. You can request a copy of an individual compiled service record by using Form NATF 86, Order for Copies of Military Service Records. You can place an order online by visiting our web site at *www.archives.gov*. If you place your order through OrderOnline!, we will receive it the next work day. You will receive your copies as soon as they are produced. If you prefer to pay by check, please use the "contact us" information to request the paper copies of the forms.

[1] Clifford Neal Smith, *Federal Bounty-Land Warrants of the American Revolution, 1799–1835* (Chicago: American Library Association, 1973).
   National Genealogical Society, *Index of Revolutionary War Pension [and Bounty-Land Warrant] Applications in the National Archives* (Washington, DC: National Genealogical Society, 1976).
[2] Virgil D. White, *Index to War of 1812 Pension [and Bounty-Land Warrant] Files*, 3 vols. (Waynesboro, TN: National Historical Publishing Company, 1989).

Searchpaths for Requests in Person

Pre-July 1908 files require name, state, land office, type of land entry, and final certificate number to locate file.

Post-July 1908 files require name and patent number to locate file.

To examine the case file of a:	Sources below index case files	Use indexing source(s) to:	Use one request slip per land file:	Submit request slip in Room G-28
Land Entry after July 1908	Two-part index: 1st part, by name, gives application number and land office...[1]	Find patent number in second part of index,[2] using appl. no. and land office obtained from first part	Fill in name of entryman and patent number	The land file will be delivered to the Central Research Room, Room 203
Land entry before July 1908 and in AL, AK, AZ, FL, LA, NV, UT	Name index for all land entries in these states only, patented and unpatented[3]	Find name of land office, type of land entry, and final certificate number	Fill in state, land office, type of land entry, and final certificate number	The land file will be delivered to the Central Research Room, Room 203
Land entry before July 1908 and in western state (see list of states below)	All land entries indexed in tract books arranged by state and legal description of land[4]	Examine tract book[5] and find land office,[6] type of land entry, and final certificate number	Fill in state, land office, type of land entry, and final certificate number	The land file will be delivered to the Central Research Room, Room 203
Land entry before July 1908 and in eastern state (see list of states below)	All land entries indexed by BLM-ESO in tract books per above and for AL, AR, FL, IA, IL, IN, LA, MI, MN, MO, MS, OH, WI, by computer	Contact BLM-ESO[7] and get copy of patent or record that shows land office, type of land entry, and final certificate number	Fill in state, land office, type of land entry, and final certificate number	The land file will be delivered to the Central Research Room, Room 203
Land entry before July 1908, and you have patent from BLM-ESO, or you know state, land office, type of entry, and file number	Then you have enough info to request pre-1908 land entries in eastern *and* western states...	....go to next box....	Fill in state, land office, type of land entry, and final certificate number	The land file will be delivered to the Central Research Room, Room 203

Western public land states: Alaska, Arizona, California, Colorado, Idaho, Kansas, Montana, Nebraska, Nevada, New Mexico, North Dakota, Oklahoma, Oregon, South Dakota, Utah, Washington, and Wyoming.

Eastern public land states: Alabama, Arkansas, Florida, Illinois, Indiana, Iowa, Louisiana, Michigan, Minnesota, Mississippi, Missouri, Ohio, and Wisconsin.

[1] RG 49, MLR# UD2137, Alphabetical Index to Case Files. Gives land office and application number.
[2] RG 49, MLR# UD2136, Numerical Index to Case Files. Arr. by land office and appl. no. Gives patent number.
[3] RG 49, MLR# UD168, Seven States Index. Gives all information needed to locate file.
[4] RG 49, MLR# UD2321, Index to Tract Books, 17 maps, available in G-28.
[5] RG 49, MLR# UD2100-2117, tract book vols. arr. by state and legal description.
[6] RG 49, MLR# UD2320, Index to Land Office, 4 vols. Available in G-28. Land office usually not given in tract book.
[7] Bureau of Land Management, Eastern States Office, 7450 Boston Boulevard, Springfield, VA 22153.

Searchpaths for Requests in Person

To examine a warrant under Act of:	Sources below index case files:	Use indexing source(s) to:	Use one reference request slip per warrant case file:	Submit request slip in Room G-28
July 9, 1788 March 3, 1803 & April 15, 1806 **Revolutionary War service**	Entire series on NARA microfilm M829, arranged alphabetically. See also published indices[1]	Examine warrant case file on NARA microfilm M829. Original records not served.	Not applicable. Original records not served. Use M829	Not applicable. Original records not served. Use M829
Dec. 24, 1811 Jan. 11, 1812 May 6, 1812 & July 27, 1842 **War of 1812 service**	Indexed and partially reproduced on NARA microfilm M848. See also published indices[2]	Determine year of warrant act, acreage, warrant number	Fill in year of warrant act, acreage, and warrant number	The case file will be delivered to the Central Research Room, Room 203
February 11, 1847 **Mexican War service**	Indexed by NARA microfilm T317 and by warrant applications ordered with NATF Form 85	Determine year of warrant act, acreage, warrant number	Fill in year of warrant act, acreage, and warrant number	The case file will be delivered to the Central Research Room, Room 203
Sept. 28, 1850 March 22, 1852 **Service in all wars since 1790, including Indian Wars**	Warrants for 1812 service indexed by NARA microfilm M313. Others by warrant applications ordered with NATF Form 85. See also published indices.	Determine year of warrant act, acreage, warrant number	Fill in year of warrant act, acreage, and warrant number	The case file will be delivered to the Central Research Room, Room 203
March 3, 1855 Service in all wars including Revolutionary War	Warrants for Rev. War service indexed by NARA microfilm M804. Others same as previous category	Determine year of warrant act, acreage, warrant number	Fill in year of warrant act, acreage, and warrant number	The case file will be delivered to the Central Research Room, Room 203

[1] Clifford Neal Smith, *Federal Bounty-Land Warrants of the American Revolution, 1799–1835* (Chicago: American Library Association, 1973).

    National Genealogical Society, *Index of Revolutionary War Pension [and Bounty-Land Warrant] Applications in the National Archives* (Washington, DC: National Genealogical Society, 1976).

[2] Virgil D. White, *Index to War of 1812 Pension [and Bounty-Land Warrant] Files,* 3 vols. (Waynesboro, TN: National Historical Publishing Company, 1989), 3 vols.

Above: The seal of the U.S. General Land Office, ca. 1861.

www.ingramcontent.com/pod-product-compliance
Lightning Source LLC
Chambersburg PA
CBHW070942290526
45795CB00003B/1119